MW01627628

Cook Books In This Series

THE WILLOW FARM PICKLE BOOK—John McKinney

THE BARMY BREAD BOOK—Jane Nordstrom

THE BREAKFAST BOOK—Kay Applegate

MORE BARMY BREADS—**Jane Nordstrom**
(LITTLE BREADS AND TEA LOAVES)

THE FIREPLACE COOK BOOK

by J. C. Lyon

THE LIGHTNING TREE—Jene Lyon, Publisher

P. O. Box 1837 Santa Fé, New Mexico 87501 U.S.A.

Cover Photograph by Margaret and John Bickel
Cover Design by Betsy James

Library of Congress Catalog Card Number: 74-77921

ISBN: (paper) 0-89016-038-4
ISBN: (cloth) 0-89016-039-2

FOURTH PRINTING

MANUFACTURED IN THE UNITED STATES OF AMERICA

THE LIGHTNING TREE—JENE LYON, PUBLISHER

Post Office Box 1837 • Santa Fé, New Mexico 87501 • U. S. A.

CONTENTS

INTRODUCTION

A woodfire in a good fireplace is like an excellent woman: bright, beautiful, warm and romantic—and baby, it can cook!

And not just a steak or a hot dog. With a little help from some handy utensils, a woodfire can cook a roast, bake a cake, simmer a soup or make a pudding. I don't claim it isn't a little trouble. It is—more trouble, at any rate, than setting a pan on a burner or popping a casserole into the oven. But you've heard of the Energy Crisis, yes? Very well then. While that cheery blaze is warming the room, it can be cooking your dinner and saving gas, electricity and money to boot.

Besides, it's rather fun. More like a picnic. A cold-weather campout with all the comforts of home. And a pleasant change of scene for the cook, who no longer has to be exiled to the kitchen. She (or he) can gather around the fire with the guests or the rest of the family, and let them help with the cooking. Let the kids or the company turn the chicken or rake up the coals around the simmering kettle. Fireplace cookery is a participating sport—any number can play. And an open fire has a lot more charm than the kitchen range. (Who wants to sit around *that* all evening?)

At our house we have a shepherd's fireplace. To tend the cooking, you have to get down on your knees and crawl under. Not exactly convenient. But it can be done and regularly is. A conventional fireplace makes things easier; though you genuflect, you don't have to crawl in. And if you have a fireplace with a raised hearth, hooray for you. You hardly have to stoop over.

Whatever its form, any fireplace will do, as long as it draws well. And you'd be surprised what a variety of dishes you can turn out with no heat but that of a bed of coals.

THE FIRE

Since you have this fireplace, you're probably familiar enough with the uses of kindling, paper and matches and need no advice on how to get a fire started. Keeping a fire may be another matter. And along this line I give you Colette's observation:

> *I am well aware of its dislike of even numbers, that three logs burn better than two and seven better than four, and that like every other animal it likes having its belly scratched from underneath.*

Three logs or seven, you will want to start your fire well ahead of cooking time and let it burn down to a good bed of coals. It's all very well for Tom Jones or Mr. Pickwick to back up to a roaring fire while a haunch of venison turns slowly above the flames. But in our fireplace cookery, flames have little use. They are merely the lovely precursors to that deep orange bed of coals where the action is. It is the coals that give you the steady heat that cooks without burning.

The best woods for this purpose are the hardwoods. Hickory, of course, is famous. Oak, maple and fruitwoods are excellent. Such woods burn slowly and not only produce good coals but contain oils and resins that lend a pleasant flavor to the foods. The trouble is, such woods are not always easily come by. In that case, you burn what you can get. We have, in our time, cooked over cottonwood, fir, black walnut, hickory, apple, cherry, the toughest locust on the Eastern shore, and Bond Street packing crates. (If you are forced to this latter choice—the use of old lumber—be aware that something happens to the board in the trip from forest to mill to lumberyard to scrap heap; something that imparts a strange taste and a tendency to much crackling, popping and an occasional small explosion. However, if nothing else is at hand, it will do.) In the Southwestern mountains where we live now, the firewood is juniper and piñon. These are quick-burning and reduce to a fine ash, and it takes some doing to get a deep bed of coals. But the piñon in particular gives an agreeable flavor, and nothing smells better in the burning.

A word of warning: For fireplace cooking, especially grilling, avoid prefabricated logs. Who knows what strange chemicals they hold! Equally assiduously avoid cooking with newspapers rolled up with those mechanical devices popular now in cities. Both these substitutes for the real thing may provide warmth and a certain cheer; what they may do to your steak or chop or well-being is dubious. On the same subject—if you use any chemical lighter, kerosene or other foreign substance to start the fire, be sure it has burned out completely before you throw a piece of meat on the grill. We have foreign substances enough in our food these days without adding any more.

THE EQUIPMENT

Let me say at the outset that we have not dealt in this book with the fireplace spit. Mostly because we don't have one. Few do. If you're one of the lucky ones, so much the better, and you probably know how to use it or you wouldn't have had it put in. Nor do we deal with the crane. Again, if your fireplace has one, you probably know by experience how hot the coals must be, how low or high the kettle that hangs above them. But until this handy Yankee invention is standard, we'll make do with simpler equipment. These are the basics:

A cast iron Dutch oven—the largest you can find, with a raised lip around the lid, so that coals can be heaped on top.

A small oven thermometer that will sit inside the Dutch oven. (Taylor makes one of stainless steel, small, relatively inexpensive, available at many hardware stores or drugstores or any good housewares department.)

Firebrick—two of these hard yellow bricks are essential, four are even better. They will support a kettle or a rack over the coals and will not crack with the heat. Available at lumberyards.

A rack for grilling—we use a heavy piece of expanded metal, sometimes called Expanded Sheet, about 12 x 18 inches. Available at lumberyards.

A large enameled iron pot with its own lid, for soups, stews and the like. (Sometimes called a Dutch oven, but known herein as a pot, to distinguish it from the big black Dutch oven proper.)

Ovenproof casserole or gratin dish that fits inside the Dutch oven. Also cake and piepans that fit.

Lots of aluminum foil.

Padded ovenmitts.

In addition to these essentials, you will find very helpful:

A long-handled, two-piece, folding wire grill—not always easy to find but sometimes available in hardware or housewares departments or with camping equipment.

A cast iron skillet with lid.

A cast iron trivet to go inside the Dutch oven.

Long-handled fork, spoon, spatula.

A pair of tongs.

Small pans, such as loaf pans; these can be foil, regular aluminum or steel.

Kabob skewers.

Poultry skewers.

A small brush for dusting ashes off the lid.

Bellows, useful also for dusting off ashes, as well as for blowing life into the fire.

And, if you're lucky enough to find one, a turkey wing for brushing the hearth.

I find it helpful, too, to have a small low coffee table or a footstool by the hearth to hold cooking implements, potholders, pitchers of basting sauce, etc.

(Since this book is concerned with energy saving, we include a note on conserving foil. Foil is extremely helpful in fireplace cooking and the heavier, the better. But this is a relatively expensive commodity and not at all inexhaustible. Aluminum is an element extracted from bauxite, which is

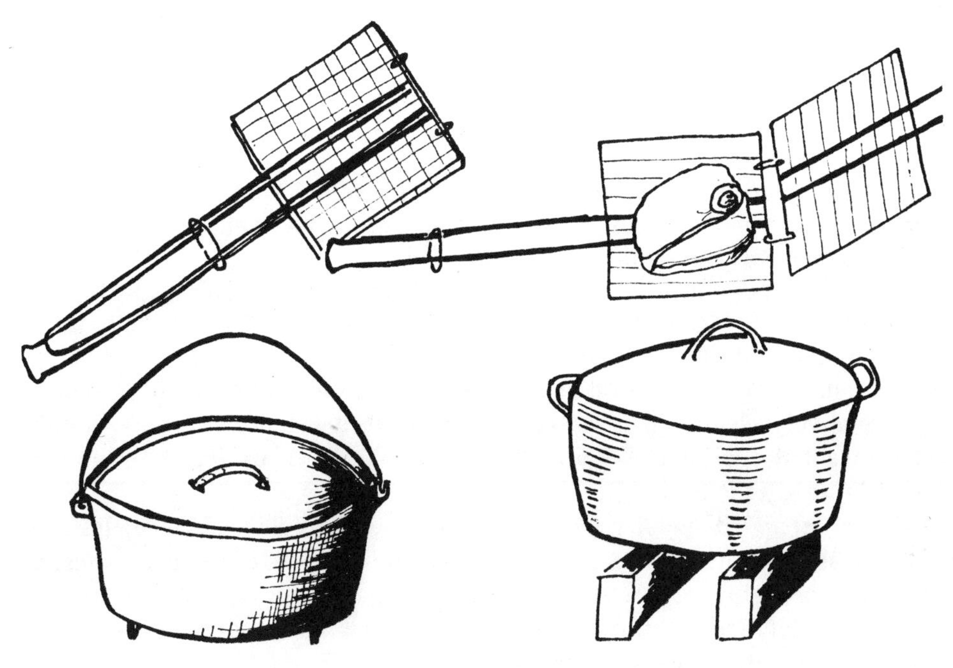

mostly imported. If the countries that supply bauxite should suddenly become difficult, as the Arabs did about oil—horrors Betsy! Even if they don't, the process of refining aluminum uses exorbitant amounts of electrical energy. So heaven forbid that we be profligate and lazy. Wash the stuff. Those big sheets of heavy foil can be washed and smoothed and re-used time after time. And when you've used them as long as patience will allow, take them to the recycling station.)

All cast iron cooking utensils have to be well seasoned to keep food from sticking. You'll probably choose to do this in the oven, though if you want to be pure, it can be done over the coals.

Warm the pot and with a clean cloth rub unsalted vegetable shortening all over the inside. (I use Crisco or any solid, unsalted shortening; oils tend to turn gummy.) Rub it in thoroughly. If black comes off on the cloth, heat the pot gently, wipe it out and rub in more shortening. Repeat till the cloth stays relatively clean. Then let the pot heat at low temperature (around 300°) for about one hour. Wipe it thoroughly with a clean dry cloth, and it should be ready for cooking.

Your expanded metal rack must also be prepared in advance. Before you lay a steak on it, or chicken or anything you broil bare, be sure to scrub the rack thoroughly with a stiff brush and hot sudsy water. There are industrial oils left from the manufacture that must be removed. When it is clean and dry rub it with shortening.

It is possible, of course, to cook soups and stews in the Dutch oven. However, I prefer to use the big enamel pot for this purpose and use the

Dutch oven for just what it is—an oven. In Colonial times this vessel was sometimes called a firepan—an accurate name, since you can set it directly on the coals or close up to a flame. With pans or ovenproof bowls that fit inside, you can bake breads, cakes and casserole dishes. Even pies. Be sure to set a trivet on the bottom to help prevent scorching. If you don't happen to have a heatproof trivet, a layer of crumpled foil will work fine.

Something else I would strongly advise: Whenever you bake in the Dutch oven—unless the inner container has its own lid or can be covered with foil, place a big sheet of foil, shiny side down, over the oven itself before you put the lid on. This is particularly important with cakes, breads or pies, and it serves two purposes. First, the aluminum reflects the heat down onto the food better than the lid alone can do; this helps brown the top. Second, it prevents what might be a very odd flavor from steam condensing on the iron lid. (Frequent washing of the Dutch oven helps, too.)

THE RECIPES

If you can broil a good cut of steak on a charcoal grill, you can broil it in the fireplace. As for hot dogs, we assume you have already done these every way there is. And of neither need any more be said.

Nor is there much to be said about the heating of pre-cooked foods, such as a can of pork & beans or a canned soup dumped in a saucepan. You can *heat* anything in a fireplace, the same as over a campfire. We're concerned less with such simplicities than with actual cooking.

The most usual way to cook over an open fire is rack-broiling, which takes, in general, the least amount of time. Probably the easiest thing is kettle cookery, which takes the longest. A big pot of soup or stew can sit on the firebrick and simmer along for hours with a minimum of tending. You will find that a good many of our recipes fall into this classification. But since it is possible to broil, boil, fry or bake in a fireplace, we have tried to give you a little of everything.

We hope you will keep in mind that for the most part our recipes are for-instances—the starting point from which you can take off on your own, adding to, leaving out, adjusting to your own tastes. If, for instance, you don't care for our Hambone-Bean Soup, your own bean soup recipe should work quite as well. Or your own Orange-Date-and-Whatnot Loaf instead of our Pineapple Bread. Since it is my feeling that salt cooked into meats or vegetables does odd things to them, I rarely salt anything until just before serving. You may wish to add salt at the first. And you don't *have* to put lemon in everything, as I tend to do. (But you'll be sorry!) The combination of ingredients is usually less important than the method of cooking. And the method, once we've given you ours, is something you will, after a bit of trial and error, no doubt, vary to suit yourself.

You will notice that a number of dishes are done in two stages, started over one evening's fire and finished over the next. Most of us tend to have a fire only at night, and certain foods, such as beans, need long slow cooking, more than there is time for in a single evening. (Unless you sit up till all hours, as we've been known to do, and don't give a hoot what time you eat.) If you happen to keep the fireplace going all day, that's another matter.

Also, certain dishes are started at the kitchen stove. Where meat must be seared or milk scalded or butter melted, it is simply quicker and easier to do so over a burner. It doesn't have to be; in case the electricity goes off or you run out of gas, all these things can be done at the fireplace.

Most meat and poultry recipes call for marinating. This improves flavor and texture and helps keep foods moist over the open heat. Times given are for marinating at room temperature. Foods put into the refrigerator should marinate overnight.

Proportions are mostly for four of normal appetite, though big kettles of soup or the like will probably feed more.

For all recipes we have given approximate cooking times. Please do keep in mind that these are *approximate*. There is no way to say precisely how long a given dish must cook. So much depends on the fire and whether you cook directly on the coals, at the edge or on a rack. You may have to burn a thing or two before you find out how long it takes. And we can not emphasize too strongly that you have to open the pot or the packet or whatever contains the food and look in on it. Frequently. It is simply not possible to set the kettle on the coals and go off to your class in ikebana. With fireplace cooking, somebody has to be there—to hover over, lift the lid, peer in, turn the pot, raise the rack, and keep the home fires burning.

But what a nice way to keep warm and get your daily exercise and save Energy! As long as you have a fireplace, and as long as you're going to light a fire for cheeriness and warmth, you may as well put the kettle on and cook a supper dish.

Some people want nothing more in a hamburger than ground beef. Not I. It is a constitutional impossibility for me to make a hamburger plain. I put things in (see Variations). But here, about as basic as I can make it is

HAMBURGERS: BASIC

ground chuck (about ¼ lb per serving)
dry red wine or ice water
bacon (1 strip per hamburger)
fresh ground pepper
salt

- In a large bowl loosen ground beef with a fork and add enough red wine (port, claret, anything good enough to drink), or ice water, to moisten meat slightly and make it cling together. It should not be sloppy. Add pepper.
- Shape into medium-firm balls and wrap each with a strip of bacon. Fasten bacon with two or three small skewers stuck completely through the hamburger and flatten the ball into a patty about one inch thick (or leave it a bit thicker if you want it rarer). The bacon should mold up around the edges, helping hold the hamburger together.
- If you use a rack over firebrick, have the coals low. If you use a folding grill, prop it against the fireplace wall, a good distance up from medium coals. The hamburgers should broil slowly enough to cook the bacon through. (It doesn't have to be burnt to a crisp but should at least be transparent and browned at the edges.) If you like your hamburgers rare, keep the rack higher above the coals.

CHEAPSTEAKS

For these we use the long, narrow, tapering strips of lean (often called chicken steaks) that lie nearest the bone in a blade cut chuck roast or chuck steak. We carve this strip from each roast and freeze them till enough accumulate for a meal. You can also use round steak cut in strips 2 or 3 inches wide and 5 or 6 long.

1 or 2 strips of beef per serving
marinade
2 jiggers of Cointreau
salt

- Pound steaks until they are as thin as you can get them. If frozen, thaw before pounding. If the meat is very thick, slice it in half lengthwise to make 2 servings. Marinate 2 to 4 hours.
- Broil on a rack over medium coals for 2 to 3 minutes per side. Since the steaks are thin, they take very little cooking. But since they may not start out as the tenderest cut, they should be well done.
- Transfer steaks to a platter and keep them warm by the fire. Heat marinade in a skillet over the fire or a burner till vegetables are wilted, 2 or 3 minutes. Add Cointreau and heat, stirring for a few seconds.
- Salt the steaks, pour sauce over them, and serve at once.

MARINADE:

4 tbsps chopped chives or green onion tops
3 tbsps chopped parsley
2 to 4 tbsps olive oil
1 tsp Worcestershire sauce
dash of Tabasco sauce

• I find the bacon provides flavor enough without extra salt. You may prefer more. If so, salt just before serving. Or every man for himself.

HAMBURGERS: VARIATIONS

These can be wrapped in bacon or not; you can leave out some ingredients and substitute others. Anything goes, if you like it. Broil the same as Hamburgers: Basic.

1. With SOYBEANS: Mix cooked, mashed soybeans with ground beef (about 1 tablespoon per serving of meat). Add a little catsup and wine, enough to make the soybeans and beef stick together. You may want to add a dash of celery seed, some chopped green chile, or any herb that suits your taste. Shape into patties, with or without bacon.

2. With BREAD CRUMBS: To one pound of ground beef add ½ to ¾ cup of dry, coarse crumbs. Moisten with catsup and wine. Add 1 teaspoon curry powder and mix well.

3. STUFFED HAMBURGERS: Use the ground beef straight or moisten slightly with wine. For each serving make 2 thin, flat patties and sandwich between them any of the following or a combination:

a slice of green chile pepper
a thin slice of Swiss cheese spread with chile sauce
a slice of sharp cheddar
a tablespoon or so of ricotta with a sprinkle of paprika and lemon juice
a thin round of sweet white or red onion.

Pinch edges of the 2 patties firmly together to keep filling from oozing out.

BROILED CHUCK ON THE COALS

We know a lady who broils a thick chuck steak on charcoal; no rack—right on the briquets. We tried it on wood coals. It works. The surface next to the heat sears almost instantly; the inside stays moist. And surprisingly, the ashes blow off and leave no grittiness.

chuck steak, 2 or 3 inches thick
marinade
salt

- Rinse the meat, drain, and if necessary use poultry skewers to hold it firmly together. Place in marinade for at least 4 hours or rest of the day.
- Let a good roaring fire burn down to thick, hot coals. Rake coals into a compact level bed and boldly place the meat directly on them.
- Sear for 2 or 3 minutes and turn. Broil the second side for 10 or 15 minutes; turn and broil the other side for the same length of time. Baste occasionally with the marinade and turn another time or two. After 40 minutes to an hour, depending on the thickness of the steak, remove meat to a platter or cutting board and slice into it. If too pink, put it back on the coals for another 5 to 10 minutes per side, or as long as it needs for the doneness you prefer.
- Slice it thin across the grain and grind coarse salt over it.

MARINADE:

¼ cup dry red wine (about)
1 or 2 tbsps salad oil
1 garlic clove crushed
fresh ground pepper
a pinch of thyme, marjoram, chervil or some dried ginger root

STUFFED BEEF ROLLS

Round steak is best for this, but the chicken steaks carved from a chuck roast also work very well.

8 pieces of beef about ¼ lb each or a bit less
stuffing
⅓ cup water
½ cup red wine (to start)

- Pound beef into very thin sheets. They should be about 5 x 8 or 9 inches when pounded. Spread with stuffing, roll and fasten with toothpicks.
- Place in a shallow pan with water and wine, cover loosely with foil and bake in the Dutch oven, with coals on the lid, for an hour to an hour and a half. They should cook more or less slowly. If necessary add more wine. The liquid should thicken slightly as it cooks and there should be enough left to spoon over the beef rolls when served.

STUFFING:

2 tbsps butter
¼ cup minced onion
8 mushrooms chopped
1½ to 2 cups bread crumbs
½ tsp celery seed
½ tsp salt (or to taste)
fresh ground pepper
1 tbsp grated orange peel
2 to 3 tbsps brandy or sherry
sour cream

- In a large skillet over a burner, heat butter and wilt onion. Add mushrooms, cover and cook slowly for 2 or 3 minutes.
- Turn off heat and add rest of ingredients, using enough sour cream to moisten the mixture and make a good spreadable paste. (You can substitute sweet cream, if you like, or yogurt or buttermilk.)

SWISS STEAK WITH VEGETABLES

2 lbs round steak
flour
1 tsp paprika
2 tbsps cooking oil
½ cup warm water
½ cup red wine
1 garlic clove
1 small head cabbage
8 small whole carrots
salt

- Wash the steak, pat dry and pound flour into it along with the paprika. Cut it into serving pieces.
- Over the stove burner, heat cooking oil in large enamel pot and brown the steak quickly. Set the pot off the burner and let it cool a few minutes.
- Add the warm water, wine and garlic clove.
- The pot is now ready for the fireplace. Set it on firebrick or a rack over low coals. It should not boil but barely simmer for about 1 hour. If it cooks too quickly, move it back from the heat or rake the coals from under it till it simmers down. And you may need to take your spatula and lift the meat from the bottom now and then to prevent sticking. Add liquid if needed.
- Meanwhile, cut the cabbage into wedges or shred the head very fine. Scrub carrots; if too large, cut in half lengthwise. When steak has cooked for about an hour, add cabbage and carrots, being sure the pot isn't dry.
- Cook for another 45 minutes to an hour. Salt to taste.

MEATLOAF

Don't yawn—this one's different.

1 lb ground chuck
¼ lb country sausage
1 egg unbeaten
½ cup chopped tomatoes, fresh or canned
⅓ cup milk (about)
¼ cup dry rice
¼ cup bread crumbs
¼ cup celery chopped fine
½ cup chopped onion
¼ lemon or ½ lime chopped, rind and all
1 tsp mustard seed
½ tsp curry powder
a grind or 2 of fresh pepper
1 tsp salt (about)
3 or 4 thin slices lemon or lime
⅓ cup white wine

● In a large bowl combine ground chuck and sausage. Add all the other ingredients except the lemon slices and wine and mix well. I like to get my hands into it and squish and squeeze till everything is thoroughly blended. This mixture should be sloppy. It is a crumbly meatloaf, not dry and solid. If it seems too heavy as you mix, add more tomatoes or juice or more milk. You may omit the bread crumbs if you like and add more or less of any of the seasonings. But the sloppy consistency, the tomatoes, the milk and the lemon or lime are what make this meatloaf distinctive.

● Spoon the mixture into a ring mold or a loaf pan and top with the lemon or lime slices.

● Have the Dutch oven heated to 350 or 375°. Set the pan in, on a trivet, cover the oven with foil and the lid and set it in the coals. Bake for about an hour or a little longer if the coals are low. A loaf will take longer than a ring.

- After about half an hour, siphon off the fat with a baster, pour in the wine, cover and finish baking. If you want the top to brown faster, heap a few coals on the oven lid.

VARIATIONS:

- If you leave out the sausage, you might try a layer of sliced cheddar or Swiss cheese in the center of the meatloaf.
- Or add ⅓ cup chopped raw peanuts.
- Or lay a slice or 2 of bacon on top of the loaf instead of the lemon or lime.
- Wheat germ can be substituted for bread crumbs.
- Sprinkle the meatloaf with toasted sunflower seeds a little before it's done.

BROILED PORK CHOPS

4 pork chops 1 inch thick
marinade
salt
fresh ground pepper

- Wash and drain chops and place in marinade for at least 4 hours.
- When the fire has burned down to a good bed of coals, place chops on the folding grill and prop at least 12 inches above the coals. If they brown too fast, move them higher. Baste frequently with the marinade and turn them from time to time. They should cook from 45 minutes to an hour, depending on the heat, and you may want to cut into one of them to be sure it is well done inside. Salt and pepper before serving. Note: Chops may also be broiled on the wire rack set across firebricks. But the coals should be rather low and not too close to the rack. Pork, as you know, must be cooked slowly and thoroughly.

MARINADE:

1/3 cup dry wine
1 or 2 tbsps salad oil
1 garlic clove crushed
2 tbsps slivered orange peel or 1 tsp crushed rosemary
1 tbsp onion chopped fine

ROAST PORK WITH BEER

You can use pork loin for this or pork shoulder roast. The size depends on your Dutch oven.

pork roast
1 garlic clove crushed
coarse salt
1 tbsp mixed herbs
fresh ground pepper
4 onion slices
beer

- Wash the roast and pat it dry. Rub it all over with the crushed garlic.
- Cover the bottom of your roasting pan with a light sprinkle of coarse salt. Place the pork on this, sprinkle it with herbs (I suggest a liberal inclusion of crushed rosemary) and fresh ground pepper. Top with onion slices.
- Have the Dutch oven moderately hot, about 350°. You may line the lid with foil or put a loose covering of foil over the roasting pan. Set the Dutch oven back a little from the fire, so that the pork cooks slowly.
- After about 30 minutes, baste the roast with ½ cup of beer. Cover and continue the slow roasting, turning the pot from time to time and adding a little beer every 40 minutes or so.
- A pork roast should cook from 35 to 45 minutes per pound. You will have to judge your cooking time by the heat. But I would say a 4-pound roast, e.g., should cook at least 3 hours and more if there's time, since fireplace heat can be less even than that of a stove oven. We have cooked a small roast (about 2½ pounds) for as long as 5 hours—slowly, basting frequently—and it turned out moist, mealy and luscious.

PORK CHOPS WITH APPLES AND SWEET POTATOES

This one-dish dinner can be baked in an ovenproof dish in the Dutch oven, or in a large enamel pot on a rack.

4 thick pork chops or 8 medium
salt and pepper
2 large sweet potatoes
3 tbsps lemon juice
2 tbsps chopped preserved ginger
2 large tart apples
2 tsps brown sugar
¾ cup cider

- In a hot greased skillet over a burner brown pork chops quickly. Transfer them to your bowl or enamel pot and sprinkle with salt and pepper.
- Peel sweet potatoes and cut into 8 slices, lengthwise. Lay these on top the pork chops. Sprinkle with part of the lemon juice, a little salt and the ginger.
- Scrub and core apples, cut into 8 thick rounds and place on top the sweet potatoes. Add the rest of the lemon juice, another dash of salt and the brown sugar. Pour cider over the whole works, cover and bake.
- If this is baked in the Dutch oven, cover the oven with foil, then the lid, and put a few coals on the lid. If baked in the enamel pot, set it on the rack over low to medium coals and keep at a low simmer. The dish should cook till pork is well done and sweet potatoes are tender—45 minutes to 1½ hours, depending on the heat.

NOTE: Instead of apples and cider you could use canned apricots with their syrup, or thick orange slices and orange juice.

PORK CHOPS WITH SAUERKRAUT, ETC.

1 lb sauerkraut
1 large tart apple
1 tsp caraway seed
1 cup green beans
¼ cup chopped sweet onion
4 thick pork chops or 8 medium
salt and pepper
¾ cup sauterne

- Drain sauerkraut and place in a large enamel pot. Add peeled chopped apple and caraway seed. Using 2 forks, toss it all together.
- Top sauerkraut with a layer of green beans, fresh, canned or frozen, cut in ½-inch pieces. Add onion.
- Brown the pork chops in a greased skillet over a burner. Place them on top the beans and sauerkraut. Season with salt and pepper and pour sauterne into the pot.
- Cover and cook on a rack over low coals for 45 minutes to an hour, till chops are well done. Look in occasionally to see that the pot has not simmered dry. If it has, add more wine or some of the juice from the sauerkraut.

CARNE ADOVADO (SPICED PORK)

A cousin to sauerbraten, made with pork instead of beef and marinated mostly in red hot chile.

1 tbsp olive oil
1 tbsp lemon juice
1 garlic clove crushed
1 tsp dried oregano
1 tsp salt
10 tbsps ground red chile (or 10 dried red chile pods put through the blender)
2 cups warm water
2 lbs lean pork cut in strips or chunks (or 8 thin pork chops)

- Combine olive oil and lemon juice, stir in crushed garlic and add oregano, salt and ground chile (a combination of the fine and coarse grinds works well). Stir in warm water.
- Add pork and turn till well coated with the sauce. Let it stand in a cool place for at least 24 hours. Refrigerated, it could stand for as long as 5 days.
- Place pork and sauce in an enamel pot. Cover, set on rack over the coals and bring to a boil. Then move it back a little or rake back the coals and keep it at a low simmer, stirring now and then. Add more water if needed. There should be a medium-thick sauce when done and the pork should be moist and very tender.

WARNING: This is for aficionados of *hot!*

BROILED HAM SLICES

2 slices pre-cooked or smoked ham about 1 inch thick
glazing sauce
pineapple or orange slices or thick slices of onion

- Place ham in glazing sauce about the time the fire is lighted.
- When flames are low and there is a good bed of coals, place ham in a folding grill and prop it well above the fire. (Or place it on your wire rack across firebrick; but be sure it does not cook too fast.) Broil it for 15 to 20 minutes per side, turning every 5 or 10 minutes and basting with the remaining sauce. Smoked ham may take a bit longer.
- When ham is done and beginning to glaze, remove it from the heat and place slices of pineapple, orange or onion on the ham. Return to the fireplace and broil, with the fruit or onion toward the fire, till fruit is lightly brown and juicy or onion slices are light brown and tender.

GLAZING SAUCE:

- Beat together with a fork till well mixed:

2 tbsps frozen orange juice, undiluted
2 tbsps white wine
2 tsps prepared mustard
2 tsps syrup from preserved ginger (or ½ tsp powdered ginger)

KIDNEYS IN BACON

This uses beef, lamb or veal kidneys separated into segments or "knobs". The number of kidneys depends on the number of servings you need.

kidneys
marinade
prepared mustard
bacon slices
salt
mustard sauce

● Separate kidneys into "knobs", probably 3 or 4 per person. Marinate for 1 to 2 hours or overnight in the refrigerator.

● Smear each knob with prepared mustard (I prefer Dijon or a Dijon-style), and wrap it in ½ strip of bacon, fastened with a toothpick or skewer.

● Place kidneys on folding grill (or on rack across firebricks), 10 inches or so above coals. Bacon should cook slowly. Broil 15 to 20 minutes, turning a time or two. Serve with mustard sauce.

MARINADE:

¼ cup salad oil
½ tsp dried basil
½ cup dry red wine
fresh ground pepper

MUSTARD SAUCE:

2 tsps chopped shallot
2 tbsps butter or margarine
½ cup sweet vermouth
2 tbsps lemon juice
½ tsp powdered mustard
salt to taste

● Heat shallot in half the butter for 1 minute. Add vermouth and simmer 2 minutes. Add lemon juice, remove from heat and swirl in rest of butter. Add mustard and salt. Pour over kidneys before serving.

BAKED CHICKEN IN FOIL

1 frying chicken
3 tbsps Worcestershire sauce
juice of 1 lemon (or more)
2 tbsps chopped onion
fresh ground pepper
1 tsp dried tarragon or oregano
salt

● Cut chicken into serving pieces and place it on a double thickness of heavy foil. You may want to make 2 packages, depending on the size and number of pieces.

● Sprinkle chicken with Worcestershire sauce, lemon juice, onion, pepper and herbs. Bring foil up around it and make a tight double fold at the top, leaving room for steam expansion.

● Bake directly on the coals, turning frequently. After 30 minutes or so, remove from the fire, open it carefully and look in on the chicken to see how it's doing. If it's too dry add more lemon juice or a little water or sherry or white wine. Reseal and finish cooking. Salt just before serving.

BROILED CHICKEN

frying chicken, quartered or cut in pieces
marinade
salt

● Wash chicken pieces and place in marinade for several hours, turning from time to time.

● When flames die down and you have a good bed of coals, place chicken in the folding grill and prop against the fireplace wall, about 18 inches above the coals. The chicken should cook slowly for 45 minutes to an hour or even longer—till the outside is brown and crisp and the inside tender. Turn it every 10 minutes or so, basting with the marinade. Salt just before serving.

MARINADES:

I.

juice of 1 to 3 limes or lemons
1/3 cup peanut oil
1/4 cup onion chopped fine
fresh ground pepper
1 tsp dried tarragon (or 1 tbsp minced fresh)
1/2 tsp Worcestershire sauce

NOTE: You might want to increase the amount of this marinade—it makes a delicious gravy with the addition of sliced mushrooms, a few peas, some cornstarch mixed with sherry, and enough water to make a medium-thick roux. Serve it with hot boiled rice.

II.

1 cup orange juice, fresh or frozen
1/3 cup salad oil
1 small garlic clove crushed
1 tbsp soy sauce

III.

⅓ cup honey
juice of 1 lemon
1 tsp powdered ginger

Mix well and smear over all sides of chicken pieces. Chicken will turn black on the outside as it broils, but the inside will stay moist and tender.

CHINESE CHICKEN IN ENVELOPES

This is Bird at its best—moist, tender chunks with a flavor that is something more than the sum of the parts.

2 whole chicken breasts boned
8 tbsps soy sauce
2 tsps honey
4 tbsps sherry (or more)
½ tsp powdered ginger

- Cut chicken breasts into 24 pieces. Mix rest of ingredients and place chicken in the sauce for one hour or more.
- Using a double thickness of heavy foil, make 4 envelopes about 6 x 6 inches; they must be sufficiently large to leave room for steam expansion as the chicken cooks. Place 6 chunks of chicken in each envelope, divide the sauce among them and seal tops with a tight double fold. (Remember the steam—leave room for it.)
- Place envelopes directly on low coals and turn them frequently. As they begin to swell, pierce the top of the envelope with a small skewer. (Only the top—you don't want to lose the sauce.) They should cook about 25 minutes.

STUFFED CHICKEN BREASTS

4 whole chicken breasts, boned and halved
4 tbsps melted butter
stuffing
4 tbsps white wine
salt

● Place boned chicken between sheets of waxed paper and pound till quite thin. Dip in melted butter.

● Spread about 2 tablespoons of filling over each half, roll up and fasten with toothpicks.

● Place 2 rolls on a double thickness of heavy foil large enough to make an envelope. Bring it up around the chicken, add 1 tablespoon of white wine to each envelope and a little of the butter remaining. Seal securely with a double fold, leaving room for steam.

● Place envelopes on the coals and bake for about 30 minutes, turning frequently. If packets swell up and threaten to explode, pierce with a skewer. Salt chicken lightly before serving.

STUFFING: (for 8 halved chicken breasts)

I.

1 cup cooked spinach, squeezed dry and chopped
½ cup pine nuts or chopped pecans or walnuts
4 tbsps grated Parmesan
¼ cup lemon juice
2 tbsp Worcestershire sauce
½ tsp salt (about)
fresh ground pepper

II.

1 cup cooked flaked crabmeat
1 tsp ground red chile pepper
3 tbsps cream (about)
¼ tsp salt (about)

III.

1 cup cooked ground ham
½ cup sour cream
⅛ tsp powdered cloves
1 tbsp orange liqueur

IV.

1 cup diced mushrooms sautéed in 2 tbsps butter
½ cup cream sauce
2 tbsps sherry
1 tsp soy sauce
⅓ cup celery chopped fine
¼ tsp salt (about)

V.

2 medium tomatoes chopped
2 tbsps minced onion
1 small garlic clove crushed
1 tbsp chopped green pepper
¼ tsp sugar
dash of pepper
½ tsp salt

Cook these together till they make a medium-thick, spreadable sauce. Taste for salt and correct if needed.

VI.

1 cup chopped dried apricots
⅓ cup water (about)
⅓ cup chopped nuts
1 tbsp brandy or orange liqueur

Stew apricots in water until they are soft and water mostly cooked out. Add nuts and brandy. You may want to salt the chicken breast lightly before spreading with this stuffing.

CORNISH HENS—BROILED

2 Cornish game hens
4 tbsps butter or margarine
2 tbsps lemon juice
1 tsp marjoram
pepper and salt

- Split Cornish hens, wash and pat dry with paper towels.
- Melt butter in small saucepan, add lemon juice, marjoram and a grind of black pepper. Stir well and brush both sides of the chickens liberally with the mixture.
- Grease the broiling rack and set it on 4 firebrick (2 stacked up at each end) over the coals. Place hens on the rack and broil for 40 minutes, more or less, turning frequently and basting with the rest of the butter sauce. If they are cooking too fast, rake back the coals. Salt before serving.

NOTE: If hens are very small, you may want to serve 2 halves per person and double the rest of the recipe accordingly.

CORNISH HENS—ROASTED

4 Cornish game hens
a cut lemon
salt and pepper
stuffing

- Wash hens, rub with cut lemon, salt and pepper, and fill lightly with stuffing.
- Wrap each hen in a double thickness of heavy foil, sealing the edges tightly but leaving room for steam expansion.
- Roast on wire rack 6 to 8 inches above low coals for 1½ hours, more

or less, turning frequently. Or bake them in the Dutch oven set in the coals, with foil under the lid and coals on top. This should take about the same amount of time.

- Test for doneness as you would chicken or turkey in the oven—by gently moving a drumstick; if it feels loose, chances are it's cooked through.

STUFFING: (for 4 hens; increase by number of hens needed)

1 cup dried apricots
water
4 tbsps chopped celery
2 tsps chopped onion
4 tbsps melted butter or margarine
2 cups dry bread crumbs
1 tsp poultry seasoning
1 tsp salt
1 tbsp brandy
¼ tsp white pepper

- Simmer apricots about 5 minutes in water barely to cover. Drain, reserving water, and chop.
- Wilt celery and onion in 1 tablespoon of the butter; do not brown them.
- Have bread crumbs ready in a large bowl. I use both white and whole-wheat bread and consider leftover biscuits and a little cornbread essential to a decent dressing.
- Combine all ingredients including water reserved from apricots. The stuffing should be crumbly, buttery, and none too moist. Too much liquid makes a slick, soggy stuffing. If you feel it is too dry, add more melted butter.

CHICKEN KABOBS

2 whole chicken breasts, boned and halved
8 small white onions
12 cherry tomatoes
marinade

- Cut chicken breasts into 16 pieces and marinate for 1 to 2 hours.
- Meanwhile, parboil onions. They should be just tender enough to skewer without falling apart.
- Thread chicken chunks on 4 steel skewers with the onions and tomatoes.
- Grease the wire broiling rack and set it on 4 firebrick (2 at each end, one on top of the other) over the coals. If the coals are too thick and hot, rake them back a little. The kabobs should cook slowly.
- Turn frequently, basting with the remaining marinade, and broil for about 20 minutes, perhaps a little longer, depending on the heat.

NOTE: This recipe works very well with 1-inch chunks of lamb.

MARINADE:

3 or 4 tbsps yogurt
1 tsp prepared mustard
½ tsp salt
1 tbsp lemon or lime juice
1 tsp chopped fresh ginger root
1 tbsp minced shallot

BROILED SHRIMP

16 raw jumbo shrimp or 24 large
juice of 3 limes
¼ cup salad oil
1 tsp paprika
fresh ground pepper

- Shell, rinse and devein shrimp. If you can find the real jumbo size, split them lengthwise. If merely the large economy size, leave them whole.
- Mix lime juice, oil, paprika, pepper; marinate shrimp an hour or more.
- Place on folding grill and prop above medium coals. Broil 5 to 7 minutes per side, or until lightly browned. Baste with the rest of the marinade.

SHRIMP IN BACON

24 large shrimp
2 cans tomato sauce
3 tbsps lemon juice
1 tsp powdered mustard
dash of Tabasco sauce
1 tbsp horseradish
1 tbsp Worcestershire sauce
1 tsp celery seed
½ tsp salt, or to taste
8 slices bacon (about)

- Shell, wash and devein the shrimp.
- Mix the rest of the ingredients and simmer in a saucepan until medium thick. Reserve ½ cup of the sauce and chill the rest.
- Dip shrimp into the warm sauce and wrap each one in bacon (⅓ of a slice should do it). Fasten with toothpicks.
- Place shrimp on folding grill, prop about 12 inches above coals and cook slowly, turning often till bacon is browned. Serve with chilled sauce.

BAKED FISH IN RED SAUCE

Red Snapper is lovely, baked in this manner, but a snapper large enough for four hardly fits in the Dutch oven. Sole, halibut or flounder fillets are a good compromise.

1½ cups tomato sauce or juice
½ cup sliced carrot
⅓ cup chopped celery
⅓ cup chopped onion
salt to taste
½ cup fresh or frozen peas
1½ to 2 lbs fish fillets
½ lemon sliced thin
fresh ground pepper

● In a saucepan combine all ingredients except peas, fish, lemon and pepper. Bring to a boil over a burner and simmer 8 or 10 minutes. The carrots should not be mushy. Add peas, cook for another 2 minutes and remove from heat.

● Rinse and drain the fillets and place in a buttered gratin dish that will fit your Dutch oven. (A pyrex plate will do.)

● Pour sauce over the fish, top with lemon slices, grind a little pepper over it, and cover the dish with foil.

● Set it on a trivet in the Dutch oven, cover and set in the coals. Cook till the sauce is bubbling and fish is tender when stuck with a fork. This should take around 20 minutes, and you'll need to give the oven a quarter turn now and then.

NOTE: This dish can be done in an enamel skillet, covered with foil or its own lid, set on a rack above the coals. Or you can cook it in foil pans wrapped in foil, set directly on the coals.

BAKED FISH IN SOUR CREAM

- 1 cup sour cream
- 1 tbsp horseradish
- 1 tsp prepared mustard
- 2 tbsps chopped parsley
- ½ tsp salt
- ¼ cup lemon juice
- dash of Worcestershire sauce
- 2 or 3 thin slices of onion
- 4 green pepper rings
- 1½ lbs fish fillets

● Mix all ingredients except onions, pepper rings and fish.

● Place onion slices in a buttered gratin dish that will fit the Dutch oven. Cover with half the fillets and spread with part of the sour cream mixture. Add the rest of the fillets, spread with rest of sour cream mixture and top with pepper rings. There should be at least enough sauce to cover the bottom of the baking dish. If it seems insufficient, add more sour cream or a little milk or white wine.

● Cover dish with aluminum foil and set on a trivet in the Dutch oven. Cover the oven and set it in the coals. Bake, turning frequently, for 20 minutes or until sauce is bubbling and fillets are fork-tender.

NOTE: This dish, like the previous one, can be baked on a rack, either in an enameled skillet or foil-wrapped foil pans.

SALMON STEAKS IN FOIL

This works equally well with swordfish steaks or trout.

salmon steaks
butter or margarine
lemon juice
Worcestershire sauce
sliced onion
fresh ground pepper

- Lay each steak on a double thickness of heavy foil large enough to make a well-sealed envelope.
- On each steak place a pat of butter (about a tablespoon), a liberal squeeze of lemon juice, a dash of Worcestershire, a slice of onion and a healthy grind of black pepper.
- Seal the packet with a double fold, leaving room for steam.
- Lay packets on low coals, or on a rack 4 to 6 inches above coals. Bake, turning frequently, for 20 to 25 minutes. When packets puff up, pierce with a skewer to keep them from exploding.

BAKED POTATOES

● Scrub baking potatoes well, rub them with butter or salad oil, wrap in a double layer of heavy foil, and poke a skewer into the middle. Place them directly on a bed of coals and cook for about 1 hour, turning frequently. Test for doneness by squeezing or by poking with another skewer.

BAKED SWEET POTATOES

● Choose medium size potatoes. Scrub and oil them, wrap in a double layer of foil and stick a skewer into the middle. Lay them on the coals and turn frequently. Sweet potatoes may take as long as 2 hours, depending on the hotness of the coals. To hurry them, keep raking fresh coals up around them. But be sure to turn often to prevent burning. Test for doneness by squeezing or with a skewer.

NOTE: Sweet potatoes will cook faster if you wrap them in a wet paper towel before wrapping them in foil.

SWEET CORN IN THE COALS

● Strip the outer husks from fresh sweet corn, leaving as many of the inner husks as will stay put. Peel these down and remove the silks. Smear the ear with butter or margarine and sprinkle with pepper. Pull the husks back into place and wrap the ear in a double layer of heavy foil. Place directly on the coals and roast 15 to 25 minutes, turning frequently. After about 12 minutes, it's a good idea to pull back the foil and the husks and make sure the corn isn't scorching. It may even be done in that time.

VEGETABLES IN FOIL

- Peas, broccoli, carrots, green beans, lima beans, cut corn, asparagus—any of these, fresh or frozen, can be cooked directly on the coals or nearby.
- Place the vegetables in small aluminum loaf pans. Season with butter or margarine, pepper and whatever herbs you choose. A tablespoon of lemon juice is always a help—more if you like (I do). And you will need to add water in about the same amount you would use if cooking the vegetable in a saucepan over the burner.
- Wrap pan in heavy foil, place on low coals or on a rack across firebricks. When it bubbles, take it off the coals but leave it near the heat, or pull it forward on the rack. Let it simmer 6 to 30 minutes depending on the nature of the vegetables. Peas, *e.g.*, take 5 or 6 minutes; fresh carrots may take an hour. Take care that the vegetable does not boil dry.
- Vegetables can also be cooked in heavy foil packets. Fold a double layer of foil into an envelope, add seasoning and liquid and seal tightly, leaving room for steam. Lay them on the coals and turn frequently. When packet swells up, poke it with a skewer.

BROILED TOMATOES

- Choose firm tomatoes and slice in half. On each cut half place a pat of butter and sprinkle with pepper, a pinch of oregano, minced parsley and, if you like, a little grated sharp cheese. Wrap each half in a layer of heavy foil, leaving room for steam. Seal tightly and bake on a rack above hot coals. They may be tender within 12 minutes or take as long as 20, depending on the heat and the distance above it.

SCALLOPED POTATOES

3 cups potatoes sliced thin
2/3 cup sliced onion
2 tbsps flour
1 1/4 tsps salt
pepper
1 tsp celery seed
1 cup grated sharp cheddar or 5 or 6 slices
3 or 4 tbsps butter or margarine
1 1/2 cups milk
2 tbsps sherry
2 tbsps chopped parsley

● Butter a gratin dish or casserole that will fit into your Dutch oven. Make layers of potatoes and onion, sprinkling each layer with flour, salt, pepper, celery seed and cheese and dotting with butter. Reserve a little of the cheese for the top.

● Pour in the milk and sherry. The liquid should cover the potatoes; if it doesn't, add a little more. Sprinkle with parsley and the rest of the cheese.

● Cover with foil and place dish on a trivet in the Dutch oven. Cover and bake on a rack or across 2 firebrick, 5 or 6 inches above medium coals. You can set the Dutch oven directly in the coals, but it requires more watching and turning.

● Bake about an hour and a half, looking in now and then to make sure potatoes have not cooked dry. Add more milk and sherry if needed.

STUFFED ACORN SQUASH

2 acorn squash
butter or margarine
salt
stuffing
½ cup water

- Wash squash, split lengthwise and scrape out seeds and strings. Rub all over with butter and salt the inside lightly.
- Place squash shells in a baking dish or pan and fill with stuffing. Add water to the dish and cover it with a lid or foil.
- Set baking dish on a trivet in the Dutch oven. Set oven in the coals, heap coals on the lid and bake for about 1½ hours or until squash is tender when stuck with a fork. If it gets too dry during the cooking period, add a little water to the baking dish.

STUFFING: (Prepared at the kitchen stove)

I.

⅓ lb sausage
¼ cup chopped onion
¼ cup chopped celery
1 cup dry bread crumbs
⅓ cup white wine
Worcestershire sauce
sour cream (or tomato juice or tomato sauce)

- In a large skillet, heat sausage and crumble with a fork. Pour off fat as it cooks. Just before it begins to brown, add onion and celery. Cover skillet and turn heat very low for about 10 minutes. Uncover and let sausage brown a few minutes longer. Add bread crumbs, wine and a dash of Worcestershire sauce and enough sour cream or tomato juice to make a good moist mixture that will stick together.

II.

½ cup sliced mushrooms
2 tbsps butter or margarine
1 cup chopped cooked ham
1 cup fine bread crumbs
2 tbsps minced parsley
2 tbsps pine nuts (or chopped pecans)
⅓ cup sweet vermouth
cream, sweet or sour

● Wilt mushrooms in butter over low heat for 2 or 3 minutes. Turn off heat and add ham, bread crumbs, parsley and nuts. Mix well and moisten with vermouth and enough cream to hold things together. If you use sour cream you may want to add a little salt.

SPINACH LOAVES

Pastry:
2 cups sifted flour
1 tsp salt
½ tsp sugar
½ cup peanut oil
¼ cup cold water

Filling:
1 cup cooked, drained, chopped spinach
2 tbsps yogurt
⅓ cup grated cheddar or blue cheese
¼ cup chopped pecans
½ tsp Worcestershire sauce
dash of nutmeg
1 tsp salt or to taste

- Have the Dutch oven heating in the fireplace. It should be about 400° to start.
- In a large bowl mix flour, salt and sugar. Add oil and water together and stir with a fork. Work mixture into a ball. The dough should be light and pliable.
- Divide dough, place half of it between sheets of waxed paper and roll medium thin. I prefer an oblong shape about 8 x 10 inches.
- Mix all ingredients for the filling. If it seems a little dry, add more yogurt.
- Spread half this mixture down the middle of the rolled out dough. Moisten edges and fold over, making a sort of loaf with well-sealed edges. Be sure it fits the baking pan that fits your Dutch oven. Repeat with rest of dough and filling and place both loaves in baking pan.

• Set pan on a trivet in the Dutch oven, cover oven with foil, and put the lid on. Bake for about 10 minutes, then move oven back a little from the hottest coals, so that it cools to something like 350°. Continue baking, about 40 minutes in all. But be sure to look in now and then to make sure the crust isn't burning. It will brown beautifully, both bottom and top, but it does have to be watched. If it browns too fast, leave it uncovered for a few minutes till the oven cools; if not fast enough, heap a few coals on the oven lid.

BAKED SOYBEANS

This dish should be started the day before.

2/3 cup dried soybeans
water for soaking
4 cups fresh water (about)
1/2 cup chopped onion
1/2 garlic clove crushed
1 cup chopped tomatoes, fresh or canned, with the juice
1 cup cooked corn
1 green chile pepper chopped
4 tbsps toasted wheat germ
1 tsp oregano
Worcestershire sauce
1 1/2 tsps salt (about)
1/2 cup grated sharp cheddar

● Soak soybeans in water through the day. In the evening when the fire is going, skim off the hulls, drain, and put beans in an enamel pot with fresh water. Add half the chopped onion and the garlic and set the pot over the coals. Bring to a boil, rake back the coals or move pot back a bit from the heat and let beans simmer for about 3 hours or till tender. They should cook down, but add water if they seem too dry.

● Next evening: You can finish this dish in the same enamel pot, but it's best to remove the soybeans, wash and dry the pot and butter it well before you put the beans back in. Add to the beans all the other ingredients except the cheese and stir them together. Top with grated cheese.

● Cover the pot, set it over the coals and simmer for about 1 hour. It should cook down pretty well again but not be completely dry. If necessary, add tomato juice.

NOTE: This can also be baked in a buttered pan or casserole in your Dutch oven with foil under the lid.

BEEF STEW

This aromatic mishmash is best begun at the stove, since it is easier to brown the beef over a hot burner than over the coals. But the fireplace is fine for the long slow cooking.

bacon fat or peanut oil
2 lbs chuck in 1-inch cubes
1 cup onion chopped or sliced
½ cup chopped celery
1 large garlic clove crushed
½ lemon sliced and chopped, rind and all
1 cup dry red wine
1 small can tomato paste
1 bay leaf
Worcestershire sauce
fresh ground pepper
2 or 3 cups water, or use part cider

- In a heavy skillet heat fat and brown beef over high heat. Transfer to a large enamel pot and add rest of ingredients above.
- Cover pot and set it across 2 firebrick over low coals. Simmer 2 or 3 hours. Add liquid if needed to keep it soupy. When beef is tender add:

3 or 4 quartered potatoes
2 or 3 carrots in chunks
2 quartered turnips
and perhaps more liquid

- Bring kettle to a boil again and let it simmer for another half hour or so, until vegetables are tender. Then add:

1 cup green peas or 1 cup green beans in 1-inch lengths
2 tsps salt (about)

- Continue simmering another 5 minutes or so. Taste for salt.

CHILE A CASA LARCOMBE

A superb variation, composed by an Easterner firmly transplanted to the Southwest. This dish is started over a burner, transferred to the fireplace for long cooking, and is best begun one evening and finished the next.

1 lb ground chuck (or ½-inch chunks)
1 or 2 garlic cloves crushed
1 large onion chopped
2 cans tomatoes drained and chopped
2 cans green chile peppers chopped (or 3 or 4 cans if you can stand the heat)
3 cups cooked pinto beans
2 tsps salt
1 tsp dried oregano
pinch of coriander
fresh ground pepper
1 cup sliced mushrooms
½ can beer
½ cup dry red wine
1 tsp grated nutmeg

● Heat oil in large enamel pot. Add beef and stir over high heat till it loses its color. Dip off excess fat. Add garlic and onion and continue cooking and stirring for another 2 or 3 minutes. Add tomatoes, chile peppers, beans, salt, oregano, coriander and several liberal grinds of black pepper.

● Cover pot, set on firebricks over low coals and simmer 1 hour. Add mushrooms and simmer another half hour. Remove from fire and let sit overnight.

● Next evening add beer and wine to the pot (or use all wine or all beer). Add nutmeg, taste for salt and simmer over the coals for 15 or 20 minutes.

SWEET-SOUR CABBAGE BALLS

15 large cabbage leaves
boiling water
1½ lbs ground beef or beef and ground veal
3 tbsps minced parsley
1 small garlic clove crushed
1 tsp salt
½ tsp celery seed
fresh ground pepper
2 lumps citric acid (approx. ½ tsp) dissolved in ¼ cup warm water; or use ¼ cup lemon juice or 3 tbsps vinegar

- Choose the 12 largest cabbage leaves, cover with boiling water and let sit for 10 minutes or longer.
- Mix rest of ingredients above, divide mixture into 12 portions and roll each into a ball.
- Drain cabbage. On each leaf place one meatball, fold leaf and fasten with toothpicks. Place remaining cabbage leaves in an enamel pot or deep skillet and add the wrapped meatballs.
- Mix ingredients for sauce and pour over meatballs. Cover the pot, set it over low coals, on a rack or across firebrick, and let it simmer for an hour to an hour and a half. Taste the sauce and adjust for salt, sweet and sour. If needed, add another lump or two of citric acid dissolved in a little warm water.

SAUCE:

2 cups tomato juice or part tomato sauce
½ cup water
¼ tsp citric acid
½ tsp salt (about)
⅓ cup brown sugar (about)

DOGBONE SOUP

So called because you can use any beef bone that comes handy—regulation soup bones, knucklebones, bones carved out of a chuck roast, neck bones, shortribs or whatever. Any of them serve to make a good stock. After that, just about anything goes. And you can give the bones to the dog.

soup bones
water
onion
1 garlic clove
wine
vegetables
lemon
fresh ground pepper
Worcestershire sauce
herbs
salt

- This is another 2-evening recipe: Wash bones and place them in a large enamel pot with 3 or 4 cups of water, half a chopped onion, the garlic and ½ cup or so of dry red wine.
- Set the pot over the coals and let it simmer for an hour or more. Remove the bones and the garlic and chill the stock overnight.
- For the next step, lift off the fat and add to the stock 2 or 3 cups of chopped vegetables. I normally include carrots, celery, a turnip, maybe a little slivered cabbage, maybe a potato or 2, a can of whole tomatoes, juice and all (chopping the tomatoes as they go in). If there's broccoli on hand I may use that and leave out the cabbage or turnip.
- Slice and chop some lemon, a quarter or half or as much as you can

stand. Add pepper, a dash of Worcestershire and some herbs, fresh or dried. I use a bay leaf and perhaps a pinch or 2 of thyme or oregano.

- Set pot over the coals as before and simmer for about 1 hour or until all vegetables are tender.
- During the last 6 or 7 minutes of cooking you may want to add a half cup of frozen or fresh peas or some green beans cut in ½-inch pieces. Any leftover cooked vegetable can be added at this time. If there's no potato in the soup, you might add a few egg noodles broken up. Bring pot back to a simmer just long enough to cook the last additions. Salt to taste and serve.

NOTE: Dry beans are a good filling addition. They can be soaked overnight and cooked with the bones and right on through.

BEAN AND HAMBONE SOUP

A good dish for a long cold spell, when you keep the fire going all day. Or you can start it one night and finish it the next.

1½ cups dry beans
water for soaking
water and vegetable stock
leftover hambone, ham scraps and ham jelly
½ cup chopped onion
1 small garlic clove crushed
½ lemon sliced and chopped
1 tsp brown sugar (about)
½ cup chopped celery
1 can tomatoes
2 tbsps green chile pepper chopped
1 tsp mustard seed
salt

- Soak beans overnight in water to cover. I prefer pinto beans or limas, but any dry beans or lentils will do.
- Place beans in a large enamel pot with 4 cups of liquid (fresh water, the water they were soaked in or vegetable stock). Add the bone left from the boiled ham and whatever ham scraps you have on hand. Two or 3 tablespoons of ham jelly add richness and flavor. Add onion, garlic, lemon and brown sugar.
- Set the pot over the coals, bring it to a boil, then rake back the coals so that the beans simmer slowly for 2 to 3 hours. The soup can be finished now or the next evening.
- When beans are tender, add celery, tomatoes (chopped), green chile and mustard seed. Salt to taste (start with 2 teaspoons and take it from

there). If beans look dry, add another cup or so of water or some tomato juice.

- Return the pot to the coals, bring to a boil and let it simmer for another hour or so.
- Remove from coals and with a potato masher mash the beans to a coarse consistency. This soup should never be thin and watery with whole beans floating around in it, but a rich thick gumbo with just enough texture to give it character. Correct the seasoning at this point. It may need more salt or a bit more brown sugar, or even a dash of vinegar from the pickle jar. The point is to have it not too bland, not too tart, but something marvelous in between. Serve it in big soup bowls—with Fireplace Cornbread.

WHOLE-CHICKEN STEW WITH DUMPLINGS

1 chicken
3 or 4 cups water
½ cup dry white wine
1 cup onion sliced thin
1 cup celery in ¼-inch diagonal slices
1 cup sliced carrots
½ lemon sliced and chopped
1 tbsp brandy
½ tsp dried chervil
½ tsp dried thyme (or 1 tbsp chopped fresh)
fresh ground pepper
2 tsps salt (about)

● Wash the chicken, clean the cavity of stringy tissue and plop it into a large enamel pot with the rest of the ingredients. (I add salt just before it finishes cooking, but you can do as you like.)

● Set the pot over the coals and simmer for 1½ to 2 hours, until chicken is falling apart and the vegetables are tender. There should be a good amount of liquid left. If necessary, add more wine and/or water during the cooking.

● Remove pot from the fire and lift out the chicken; keep it hot on a platter. Dip out most of the vegetables and part of the stock. There should be about 2 inches of liquid left in the pot. Bring this to a boil and drop in the dumpling batter by cooking-spoonfuls. Cover tightly and let simmer for about 15 minutes. These dumplings will soak up most of the liquid and tend to be mushy, but they taste great. Serve in bowls with pieces of chicken and a ladleful of the soup and vegetables.

DUMPLINGS:

- 1 cup cornmeal
- 1/4 cup flour
- 1 tsp baking powder
- 1/2 tsp salt
- 1/2 tsp sugar or honey
- 1/2 tsp dried basil
- 2 eggs
- 1/2 cup buttermilk
- 1 tbsp melted butter or margarine

● Mix dry ingredients. Beat eggs lightly, add buttermilk and add to the dry mixture. Stir in melted butter. If batter seems too thin, add a bit more flour.

POSOLE

The eponym of this dish is white corn hominy made from the dried kernels with water and slaked lime. The dish is a staple among the Spanish and Indians of the Southwest, and fresh posole *is available in the chilled food case at the supermarkets. It is often cooked with pigs' feet, pork rind or ribs or beef tripe. Our Spanish version uses cubed fresh pork and beef.*

1 lb posole corn (or a large can of white hominy)
1 lb cubed fresh pork
1 lb cubed beef
1 tbsp chopped onion
1 garlic clove crushed
2 tsps salt (about)
1 tsp dried oregano
2 tbsps red chile powder (or 2 red chile pods crushed or 1 can green chile peppers chopped)
6 cups water (or part beef stock)

● Place all ingredients in a large enamel pot. Set pot over the coals and bring to a boil. Rake coals away from the pot, or raise the rack so that the pot simmers as slowly as possible. Cook for 3 or 4 hours, stirring frequently, until meat is tender and the posole has "popped". (Fresh posole still has the hulls on. Skim them off as they rise to the surface.)

NOTE: If you happen to have a fire going all day, the pot can simmer along for the whole time. This does nothing but improve the flavor. Add water or stock to keep it from going dry. The final result should be soupy.

ARROZ CON POLLO

Another dish started over a burner—though it can be done entirely over the coals.

1 frying chicken
2 tbsps cooking oil
1 large onion chopped
1 or 2 garlic cloves crushed
½ cup chopped celery
½ lemon sliced and chopped
¼ tsp crumbled saffron
2 cups canned tomatoes
1 cup tomato juice
1 cup water
½ cup dry white wine
1½ cups raw rice
1 green chile pepper chopped (or ¼ tsp red chile powder)
2 tsps salt (to start)
1 bay leaf

● Cut chicken into small serving pieces. Heat oil in a large enamel pot and brown chicken over medium high heat. Transfer chicken to a platter.

● To the fat remaining in the pot, add the onion, garlic and celery and stir over medium heat for a couple of minutes, till they are coated with fat and heated through but not brown.

● Add lemon, peel and all, saffron, tomatoes (chop them as they go in and use all the liquid) and the rest of the liquid. Bring to a boil and add rice, the green or red chile, salt and bay leaf. Give them a quick stir with a fork and return the chicken to the pot. Cover tightly.

● Set the pot over low coals and let it simmer for 1 to 1½ hours, until chicken is tender, the liquid absorbed and rice tender but not mushy. It may be necessary to stir it gently now and then to prevent scorching. If rice begins to look too dry, add more tomato juice or water or wine.

SPLIT PEA SOUP

This can be seasoned with a leftover hambone, a cup of chopped cooked ham, some ham jelly, a thick bacon rind, ½ cup of diced salt pork, browned, or any combination of these.

2 cups dried split peas, green or yellow
6 cups water (about)
a hambone (or see above)
½ cup chopped onion
½ cup chopped celery
1 garlic clove crushed and diced
¼ lemon sliced and chopped
1 medium turnip diced fine
2 carrots diced
fresh ground pepper
2 tsps salt or to taste

● Rinse split peas through several waters and put them in a large enamel pot with water. Set pot over the coals and bring it to a boil. Rake the coals back a bit and let pot simmer for about 30 minutes, stirring frequently.

● Add to the pot the hambone or any of the alternates, the onion, celery, garlic and lemon. Simmer for about 1 hour more.

● Add turnip, carrots, pepper and salt and bring the soup back to a simmer for another 30 minutes or so, until carrots are soft. Add water if needed to keep the mixture soupy.

● Now you have several alternatives: If you like a velvety soup, put it through a sieve or a foodmill. Or put it in the blender. If you like a coarser texture (I do) and don't want all the bother, take the electric beater to it right in the pot or smush it around with a potato masher. It should be a good thick soup, a meal in itself.

SPOON BREAD

- 2 cups milk
- 1 cup cornmeal
- 4 tbsps melted margarine
- 2 eggs unbeaten
- 2 tsps honey
- 1 tsp salt
- 1 cup milk
- 4 tsps baking powder

● Over a stove burner scald 2 cups of milk. Add cornmeal and stir over very low heat until thickened. Set aside and let cool for 5 or 10 minutes.

● Meanwhile, heat the Dutch oven to medium hot (350° by your thermometer).

● To the cornmeal mixture add melted margarine and stir well. Beat in the eggs. Add honey, salt and rest of milk. Add baking powder a spoonful at a time, stirring in gently. It will be a thin batter.

● Pour into buttered baking dish or loaf pan and set in the Dutch oven on a trivet. Cover oven with foil and the lid and put a few coals on the lid. Set oven over low coals and bake for about 1 hour, turning frequently. After half an hour or so, look in on it and if necessary move it back from the heat or closer in, depending on how fast it's baking. Bake till a toothpick comes out fairly clean and the top is lightly browned and a little crackled. Like any good spoonbread, it shouldn't be too dry.

BUTTERMILK BISCUITS

My mother never measured anything, but her biscuits won prizes. Here, in more measured terms, is her recipe. More or less. Though they may turn out better in a stove oven, they do very nicely in the fireplace: a medium-thin biscuit with a fragile crust and little inside but air.

2 or 3 cups flour
3 level tsps baking powder
½ tsp salt
1 tsp sugar
4 tbsps shortening
1 cup buttermilk
1 tbsp shortening for the biscuit pan

● Sift flour into a bowl, make a well in the middle and add baking powder, salt and sugar. Mix with a fork, throwing in flour from the sides.

● Add shortening (my mother used lard; I use vegetable shortening). Toss flour over it and work it with your fingers till shortening and flour are coarsely crumbled together. Make a well in the middle of this and add buttermilk. No, it takes no soda. Stir all this together with a fork till it forms a sort of ball. It probably will not take all the flour. The dough should be quite soft, only firm enough to lift out onto your floured board.

● Knead dough very briefly with the fingertips and roll out ½ to ¾ inch thick. Cut into rounds.

● Heat Dutch oven to 450°. Set your biscuit pan in it, with a tablespoon of shortening. When shortening has melted, lift out the pan with the tongs. As you put the biscuits in, dip them in the melted shortening and turn them over. Return pan to the Dutch oven.

● Cover oven with foil, put the lid on and heap a few coals on the lid. Bake 15 to 20 minutes, until biscuits are lightly browned. If the coals are too low it may take longer.

BUCKWHEAT MUFFINS

A chewy concoction, great with soups and stews.

¼ cup softened margarine
2 tbsps sugar
2 tbsps molasses
1 large egg or 2 small
1 cup buttermilk
1¼ cups sifted flour
2 tsps baking powder
½ tsp salt
½ tsp soda
½ to ¾ cup buckwheat groats
¼ cup raisins or currants

● Cream margarine with sugar and molasses, break the egg in and beat well. Add about half the buttermilk.

● In another bowl sift flour with baking powder, salt and soda. Add buckwheat groats and stir. Add this mixture to the creamed mixture, alternating with the rest of the buttermilk. Stir gently, only until dry ingredients are moistened. Add raisins, again stirring only just enough. The batter should be rather lumpy. Fill greased muffin pans about half full.

● Have the Dutch oven heated to about 425°. Set the muffins in, cover the oven with foil, put the lid on and heap coals on the lid. Bake about 30 minutes, turning frequently. Check to make sure the muffins aren't browning too fast on top. If they are, leave the coals off the lid.

KETTLE CORNBREAD

2 cups stone ground cornmeal
1 tsp soda
1 tsp salt
2 cups buttermilk
2 tbsps honey
2 eggs unbeaten
4 tbsps melted margarine or peanut oil

- Mix dry ingredients. Stir in half the buttermilk and the honey. Break eggs into mixture and beat well. Add rest of buttermilk, margarine or oil and mix well.
- Meanwhile, heat the Dutch oven in the fireplace. It should be quite hot —400-450° by your little thermometer. As it heats, set your bread pan inside it, well greased, and let it get sizzling hot.
- Pour batter into the hot bread pan and set it back in the Dutch oven on a trivet. Cover oven with foil, put the lid on and heap coals on top. Bake for about 30 minutes, turning frequently. After 10 or 15 minutes, brush off the ashes and look in on the bread. If it seems to be browning too fast, leave the coals off the lid, or move it back a little from the heat. Continue baking till top is lightly browned and a toothpick comes out clean.

VARIATIONS:

- Add to the batter any of the following or a combination:

⅓ cup wholegrain corn; a tablespoon or 2 of chopped green chile pepper; 1 or 2 chopped jalapeño peppers (watch it—they're hot!); ⅓ cup grated sharp cheese; bits of cooked pork or bacon; ⅓ cup wheat germ; ¼ cup chopped nuts.

TUNNBROD

A recipe borrowed from The Barmy Bread Book *by Jane Nordstrom, who adapted it from a spicy flat bread made in Northern Sweden and traditionally baked on a large griddle over an open fire. The Swedes wrap it around fish, cheese or smoked reindeer meat. As a substitute for the reindeer meat we suggest broiled hotdogs, hamburgers or sliced steak.*

1 tbsp or 1 pkg yeast
1 cup warm water
⅓ cup corn syrup
1½ tsps anise seed crushed
1½ tsps fennel seed crushed
1 cup mashed potato
1 tsp salt
4 tbsps margarine melted
½ cup powdered milk
1 cup rye flour
3 cups white flour (about)

- Soak yeast in warm water for about 5 minutes. Add remaining ingredients with enough white flour to make a firm dough. Knead until smooth and let dough rise for about 1 hour in a warm place.
- Punch down dough and divide into 24 pieces. Form pieces into small balls and cover lightly with plastic so they won't dry out.
- Meanwhile have a large cast iron skillet heating over low coals; it should be only medium hot. Roll the balls of dough, one at a time, into very thin sheets about 9 or 10 inches in diameter. Without letting it rise, place a sheet on the hot, ungreased skillet, prick it all over with a fork and bake for 2 or 3 minutes on each side, until lightly colored. While one sheet bakes, roll out the next. The breads should be thin and flexible.

JEWELL'S CARROT BREAD

A delicious tea bread which can be served cold or lightly toasted, with or without butter. It also makes a festive breakfast bread.

1½ cups flour
1 cup sugar
1 tsp baking soda
1 tsp cinnamon
¼ tsp salt
¾ cup cooking oil
2 eggs unbeaten
1 tsp vanilla
1 cup grated raw carrot
½ cup walnuts, pecans or black walnuts

● Mix all ingredients except the last two. Beat well, fold in carrot and nuts and pour into a buttered, floured loaf pan.

● Have the Dutch oven heated to 350°. Set the carrot bread in the oven on a trivet, cover oven with foil, put the lid on and put coals on the lid. Bake for about 1½ hours, until a toothpick comes out clean and bread is lightly browned on top. Turn the oven frequently, and look in on it a time or two to see that the top is not browning too fast. If it is, leave the coals off the lid.

JEN'S PINEAPPLE BREAD

Another of those delectable loaves to serve with morning coffee or 4 o'clock tea.

½ cup raisins
boiling water
1¾ cups sifted flour
2 tsps baking powder
½ tsp salt
½ tsp soda
¾ cup sugar
3 tbsps soft butter or margarine
2 eggs unbeaten
¾ cup chopped pecans
1 cup crushed undrained pineapple
2 tbsps sugar
½ tsp cinnamon

- Rinse raisins in boiling water to plump them. Drain well.
- Sift together flour, baking powder, salt and soda and set aside.
- Gradually beat sugar into butter. Beat in eggs one at a time. Add raisins and nuts and sift in about half the flour mixture. Stir it in gently—don't beat.
- Add pineapple with its syrup. Stir in rest of flour mixture—gently! Pour into a buttered, floured loaf pan and sprinkle with rest of sugar and cinnamon.
- Have your Dutch oven heated to 350°. Set the bread in, on a trivet, cover the oven with foil, put the lid on and put coals on the lid. Set oven in low to medium coals and turn frequently.
- After half an hour or so, brush the coals off carefully and look in on the bread to make sure it isn't browning too fast on top. If not put the coals back on and continue baking; if it is, leave the coals off. The bread will probably take an hour to an hour and a half, overall.

APPLES IN THE COALS

large baking apples
raisins
pecans or walnuts
brown sugar or honey
sherry or rum
salt
butter or margarine
sliced lemon

• Scrub and core apples. I save the bottom part of the core for plugging the hole. Stuff the core with raisins, nuts and sugar (about 1 teaspoon per apple) or dribble honey in it. Pour in about a tablespoon of sherry or rum, add a dash of salt, top with a pat of butter and a thin slice of lemon.

• Wrap apples individually in a double layer of heavy foil, leaving room for steam and sealing tightly. Set them on the coals and bake till soft when lightly squeezed (be sure to wear your ovenmitts!). This may take anywhere from 40 minutes to an hour and a half. Turn apples frequently, and pierce top of foil wrappers if they threaten to burst.

NOTE: Apples can also be baked in the Dutch oven, much the same as in a regular oven. Place them in a pan with a little water, cover lightly with foil, set the pan on a trivet and cover the oven. Set it directly in the coals or nearby and put coals on the lid or not, depending on how fast you want them to cook. Look in on them now and then to be sure they aren't scorching.

APPLE-ALMOND PIE

Crust:

2 cups sifted flour
1 tsp salt
½ tsp sugar
½ cup peanut oil
¼ cup cold water

Filling:

¼ cup sliced toasted almonds
3 cups sliced tart apples
1 tbsp flour
¾ to 1 cup sugar (brown or white)
¼ tsp salt
dash of cinnamon or nutmeg
3 tbsps lemon juice
2 tbsps butter or margarine

- In a large bowl mix flour, salt and sugar. Add oil and water together.
- Mix lightily with a fork, then work into a ball with your hands. Roll half the dough between sheets of waxed paper. Lift off top sheet, invert dough over piepan and peel off bottom sheet. Fit dough into the pan.
- Cover bottom crust with almonds and fill with apples. Sprinkle with flour, sugar, salt and spices. Add lemon juice and dot with butter.
- Roll out rest of dough between sheets of waxed paper, pierce it with a fork and drape it over the apples, crimping edges together.
- Meanwhile, heat the Dutch oven to 450°. Set the pie on a trivet inside and cover oven with foil. Put the lid on, heap coals on the lid and keep oven hot for 15 minutes, turning frequently. Then move oven back from heat to cool to about 350°. Brush off coals and look in to make sure the top isn't browning too fast. If so, leave the coals off. If not, put them back and continue baking another 30 or 40 minutes, turning frequently.

GINGERBREAD

2 cups sifted flour
2 tsps baking powder
½ tsp soda
½ tsp salt
1 tsp cinnamon
¼ tsp cloves
⅓ cup shortening
½ cup sugar
1 large egg or 2 small
¾ cup molasses
¾ cup buttermilk
2 tsps grated or chopped fresh ginger root (or 2 tsps powdered ginger)
1 tsp grated lemon rind
½ cup chopped nuts

● Sift together the flour, baking powder, soda, salt, cinnamon and cloves. (If you're using powdered ginger, add it here.)

● In a large bowl cream shortening and sugar, add egg and beat well. Add molasses and beat some more.

● Add dry ingredients alternately with buttermilk, stirring gently. Add ginger root, lemon rind and nuts and pour into a buttered, floured pan that fits the Dutch oven.

● Heat Dutch oven to 350°. Set the cake pan inside on a trivet, cover the oven with foil, put the lid on and heap coals on the lid. Bake 45 minutes to an hour, turning frequently. At some point, brush off coals and look in to see how it's going. If it's browning too fast, leave coals off the lid. If necessary, pull oven back a way from the heat. Continue baking till it passes the toothpick test.

APRICOT-ANGOSTURA CAKE

½ cup shortening
1 cup brown sugar firmly packed
1½ cups sifted flour
1 cup cooked, mashed, unsweetened apricots
1 tsp soda
½ tsp salt
1 tsp cinnamon
¼ tsp powdered cloves
1 tbsp angostura bitters
1 cup chopped raisins
½ cup chopped nuts
1 tbsp flour

- Cream shortening and sugar till fluffy and add a little flour.
- Heat apricot sauce till barely warm and stir in the soda. Add to shortening mixture alternately with rest of flour.
- Stir in salt and spices and angostura bitters. Sprinkle raisins and nuts with the tablespoon of flour and add to batter. Pour into a buttered, floured pan (square, round or loaf).
- Heat Dutch oven to 350°. Set the pan inside on a trivet, cover oven with foil, put the lid on and put a few coals on the lid. Set oven back in the coals or nearby, and turn frequently.
- After about 30 minutes, brush off the coals and look in at the cake. (Lifting the lid doesn't seem to hurt it.) If it is browning too fast on top, leave coals off the lid. Move the oven back to where it will stay at approximately 350° and continue baking. It may take an hour to an hour and a half.

NOTE: At higher altitudes (over 3000 feet), reduce sugar by 2 tablespoons and beat in an egg with the shortening-sugar mixture.

UPSIDE DOWN CAKE

Unless you have a heavy skillet with a detachable handle, that will fit your Dutch oven, you can use a regular cake pan or even a pyrex pie plate. I use two aluminum pans, 8 x 8 x 2, one inside the other, and find this works very well. For the fruit, you can use sliced pineapple, fresh or canned apricots or peaches, or stewed dried fruit (apricots, peaches, apples, even prunes, or a combination). The cake part can be your own plain cake recipe, a sponge cake, or a package mix. To start from scratch, here's my method.

TOPPING:

¼ cup butter or margarine
1 cup brown sugar
fruit
½ cup nuts
candied cherries or preserved ginger

- Melt butter in cake pan. Spread brown sugar over bottom of pan and cover with pieces of fruit, as many as you want or can fit in. Fill spaces with nuts (pecans, walnuts, black walnuts) and cherries or ginger, if you have them on hand.

CAKE BATTER:

- 1/3 cup shortening
- 1 cup sugar
- 2 eggs unbeaten
- 1 1/2 cups sifted flour
- 2 tsps baking powder
- 3/4 tsp salt
- 1 cup milk
- 1 tsp vanilla

- Cream shortening and sugar till fluffy. Add eggs and beat well.
- Sift together the flour, baking powder and salt. Add to creamed mixture in thirds, alternating with milk. You may want to use a little more flour, depending on the feel of the batter. I like it to be fairly thin; too much flour makes a dry, solid cake. Use as little as you think you can get by with. Add vanilla.
- Pour batter over the fruit-sugar mixture. Since a pan that fits the Dutch oven may be smaller than you'd normally use, you may have batter left over. Put it in a small buttered loaf pan and freeze it for baking later.
- Have the Dutch oven heated to 325-350°. Set cake in oven on a trivet and cover oven with foil. Put the lid on, put a few coals on top and set oven in the coals. Keep the heat as even as possible, and look in on the cake after about 20 minutes. If browning too fast on top, leave coals off the lid. Continue baking for another 10 to 20 minutes, or until a toothpick comes out clean.
- Turn cake upside down at once on a large plate. Serve with whipped cream or with sour cream lightly sweetened and flavored with a dash or two of angostura bitters.

FRUIT PUDDING

For this steaming dessert almost any tart fruit or combination of them will do: apples, peaches, apricots, plums, cherries, pineapple, or whatever—fresh, canned or frozen.

2 or 3 cups of fruit
½ cup brown sugar (about) or honey to taste
salt
lemon juice
2 or 3 tbsps liqueur
2 cups cubed leftover cake
sour cream
a little sugar

● Peel, slice or chop the fruit, add the half cup of sugar, more or less, depending on your taste and the tartness of the fruit, a dash of salt, a liberal squeeze of lemon and the liqueur. I prefer Cointreau or Grand Marnier or any of the orange or cherry flavors. Or you may substitute rum or vanilla. Add cake cubes and mix lightly.

● Pour mixture into a buttered baking dish, cover lightly with foil and put in Dutch oven on a trivet.

● Set oven on or near the coals, cover and let simmer 5 to 10 minutes, until fruit is tender and juicy. If necessary, add liquid (more of the liqueur, orange juice, cider or plain water) to keep mixture moist. Serve hot or cold with a dollop of lightly sweetened sour cream.

NOTE: This dish can be made without the cake. Serve it plain or spooned over slices of pound or angel cake.

STRAWBERRY BETTY

We have a beautiful, worldly friend who grew up in a Tennessee cotton patch. She writes that her grandmother baked pound cake in the fireplace (as well as rabbit, squirrel, possum and cornpone). The cake was cut into small squares, speared on a thin, peeled stick, dipped into rich cream, then into damson plum preserves, held over the coals till hot, and eaten at one bite. At Christmas, to gild the already pure gold lily, they dipped the cream-and-damsoned cake bites into grated fresh coconut.

We've tried it—using half-and-half instead of thick Jersey cream, and strawberry jam instead of damson (damsons being scarce these days). Though the cake tends to crumble and the jam drips, it is a delicious morsel.

More practical perhaps is this adaptation, done in a baking dish:

sliced angelfood cake
strawberry jam
sour cream
chopped nuts
slivered toasted fresh coconut

- In a well-buttered baking dish make a layer of angelfood slices. Spread with sour cream and dribble jam over the cream. Sprinkle with nuts. Make another layer of cake, jam and sour cream. Top this with toasted coconut.
- Set dish on a trivet in Dutch oven and cover oven with foil. Put the lid on and coals on the lid. Set in the coals and bake for 15-20 minutes, till mixture is steaming.

BESSIE SPRINKLE'S BREAD PUDDING

3 cups bread crumbs
1 cup sugar
½ cup butter or margarine
2 eggs
1 cup milk
1 tsp soda
1 tbsp warm water
1 tsp cinnamon
½ tsp ground cloves
1 tsp salt
1 cup raisins
½ to 1 cup chopped nuts

- Unless you happen to have plenty of bread crumbs on hand, heat sliced bread in a slow oven till very dry and crumbly. Grind or blend it to the consistency of coarse meal.
- Cream together sugar and butter. Add eggs and beat well. Add milk alternately with bread crumbs.
- Dissolve soda in warm water and add to mixture. Stir in spices and salt and fold in raisins and nuts.
- Ideally, this should be steamed in a 1-pound coffee can, one of the old ones about 5 inches high. If you have no round tin that will fit the Dutch oven, use a buttered baking dish or pan, as deep as will fit. With foil make a loose tent over the container so the steam doesn't condense too much on the pudding.
- Set in the Dutch oven, with water to come about half way up the sides of the pudding dish or pan. Cover the oven and set it over very low coals. When water begins to simmer, move it back and keep at a simmer for about 3 hours, until pudding has a soft, cake-like consistency.
- Remove from oven, let cool and remove from container. Wrap in waxed

paper to keep moist and store in refrigerator. To serve, cut in slices and top with hard sauce.

HARD SAUCE:

1 cup powdered sugar
3 tbsps softened butter
1/8 tsp salt
1 or 2 tbsps cream
1 tsp lemon extract

● Sift sugar over softened butter a little at a time, stirring with each addition. Add rest of ingredients and beat until well blended. If it's too soft, add more sifted sugar. The mixture should be about the consistency of pie dough.

● Turn out on waxed paper, shape into a roll and chill. Serve a slice of sauce over each slice of pudding.

NOTE: You may substitute other flavoring for the lemon extract. But I warn against fresh lemon juice: according to Miss Bessie, the fresh juice makes the sugar crusty.

ROASTED CHESTNUTS

- It is often a good idea to soak Italian chestnuts in hot water for 30 minutes or so just before roasting. Drain well.
- An English chestnut roaster is the ideal implement. This is a shallow perforated pan with a prudently long handle (chestnuts tend to explode). These roasters are often available in the housewares department of the larger stores. But if you do not have one, use a cast iron skillet.
- Heat the chestnuts over the coals till they begin to steam (or until one of them explodes). Transfer them to a wooden bowl and let cool until they can be handled. With a knife for cutting the shell, everybody can peel his own. Salt and eat them hot.

TOASTED WALNUTS

- Place unshelled English walnuts in a heavy skillet and set on a rack over medium coals. Heat for about 10 minutes, stirring frequently with your long-handled spoon or spatula. Dump them into wooden bowls and serve with nutcrackers, salt, chilled crisp apples and glasses of Madeira or port.